DAYS OF
DECISION

Bush, Blair, and Iraq

Heinemann
LIBRARY
Chicago, Illinois

Andrew Langley

Edited by Andrew Farrow, Adrian Vigliano, and Mark Friedman
Designed by Cynthia Della-Rovere
Original illustrations © Capstone Global Library Ltd.
Illustrated by H L Studios and Cynthia Della-Rovere
Picture research by Elizabeth Alexander
Production by Sophia Argyris

Originated by Capstone Global Library Ltd
Printed in China by RR Donnelley South China

17 16 15 14 13
10 9 8 7 6 5 4 3 2 1

Library of Congress Cataloging-in-Publication Data
Langley, Andrew, 1949-

  Bush, Blair, and Iraq / Andrew Langley.

    pages cm.——(Days of decision)

  Includes bibliographical references and index.

  ISBN 978-1-4329-7633-0 (hb)—ISBN 978-1-4329-7640-8 (pb) 1. Iraq War, 2003-2011—Causes—Juvenile literature. 2. Bush, George W. (George Walker), 1946—Juvenile literature. 3. Blair, Tony, 1953—Juvenile literature. I. Title.

  DS79.757.L36 2013

  956.7044'31—dc23   2012041473

Acknowledgments
The author and publishers are grateful to the following for permission to reproduce copyright material: Corbis pp. 4 (© Brooks Kraft), 11 (©Rick Maiman/Sygma), 13 (©Bettmann), 19 (©Brooks Kraft), 20 (©Reuters), 24 (©Kevin Lamarque/Reuters), 36 (©Atef Hassan/Reuters), 38 (©Handout/Reuters), 41 (©STR/epa), 50 (©Mario Tama/POOL/epa), imprint page (©STR/epa); Getty Images pp. 7 (Dirck Halstead/Time Life Pictures), 9 (INA/AFP), 5 (Michel Gangne/AFP), 28 (Scott Barbour), 37 (Benjamin Lowy), 40 (Sabah Arar/AFP), 43 (Muhannad Fala'ah), 46 (Adek Berry/AFP); Photoshot pp. 22 (WpN/UPPA), 45 (Photo Researchers); Rex pp. 16 (Sipa Press), 33 (Chris Balcombe), 35 (Shinichi Murata), 49 (Mark St George); U.S. State Department p. 26.

Background and design features reproduced with the permission of Shutterstock (©Picsfive, ©Petrov Stanislav, ©Zastolskiy Victor, ©design36, ©a454).

Cover photograph of President George W. Bush and UK Prime Minister Tony Blair holding a news conference in 2004 reproduced with the permission of Getty Images (Ken Cedeno/Bloomberg via Getty Images); Cover photograph of U.S. Army soldiers moving down an enemy trench reproduced with the permission of Getty Images (Scott Nelson/Photonica World).

We would like to thank Dr. John Allen Williams for his invaluable help in the preparation of this book.

Every effort has been made to contact copyright holders of any material reproduced in this book. Any omissions will be rectified in subsequent printings if notice is given to the publisher.

Contents

Some words are printed in **bold**, like this. You can find out what they mean by looking in the glossary on page 60.

Fighting Saddam

On March 20, 2003, armed forces from the United States, the United Kingdom, and other countries invaded Iraq. Their aim was to get rid of the Iraqi leader, Saddam Hussein, and to bring peace and **democracy** to the country. Within a few weeks, the invaders had taken control of Iraq, and Saddam was in hiding. But the war was not over. It dragged on for another eight years, until late 2011, and became one of the most controversial conflicts since World War II (1939–1945).

Bush and Blair

U.S. President George W. Bush was the person who made the final decision to send U.S. soldiers into Iraq. On the night of March 19, 2003, he announced that the United States had gone to war. In a televised speech, he said, "American and **coalition** forces are in the early stages of military operations to disarm Iraq, to free its people, and to defend the world from grave danger."[1]

By far the biggest part of the invasion force was American. Altogether, there were over 240,000 U.S. military personnel involved (about 80 percent of the total).[2] Another 45,000 troops came from the United Kingdom. UK **Prime Minister** Tony Blair was Bush's most loyal supporter throughout the long buildup to war.

George W. Bush (right) and Tony Blair (left) believed passionately that a military invasion of Iraq was the only possible way of forcing Saddam Hussein from power.

For and against the war

Bush and Blair made decisions that led their countries into war with Iraq because they believed Saddam Hussein posed a threat to his neighbors and to world stability. Their aim was to **liberate** Iraqis from the rule of a dangerous **dictator** and to help the Iraqi people build a democratic system of government, which would allow them to choose their own rulers. This book examines those decisions, as well as the **legacy** these decisions created for the two leaders—and for the world.

Other people believed the invasion was a big mistake. Governments in many countries in Europe and Asia opposed the conflict. The Security Council of the United Nations (UN) did not think the war was justified. During early 2003, millions of ordinary people across the world took part in demonstrations protesting against the planned attack on Iraq.

Saddam Hussein 1937–2006

Born: Al-Awja, Iraq

Role: President of Iraq, 1979–2003

Saddam Hussein was born into a poor family near Tikrit, in northern Iraq. In 1957, he joined the Ba'ath Party, which was then a small **Sunni** organization struggling for power. (Sunnis are a minority **Muslim** group in Iraq.) But by the late 1970s, the Ba'ath Party ruled Iraq, and Saddam had risen to be a leading politician. In 1979, he became Iraq's president. He immediately killed or imprisoned his rivals, to make sure no one would challenge him. Despite such brutality, he used Iraq's oil revenue to build schools and hospitals and installed electricity across the country.

From 1980 to 1988, Saddam fought a costly war against neighboring Iran. He also used enormous violence against his opponents at home. For example, in 1988, his air force dropped poison gas on the **Kurdish** town of Halabja, killing over 5,000 people.[3] Two years later, Saddam launched an invasion of the small neighboring country of Kuwait.

Did you know? During Iraq's war against Iran in the 1980s, Saddam received support from Western countries, including the United States and the United Kingdom. He was seen as an important ally against the growing power of Iran, which had become hostile to the United States after an **Islamic** revolution (see page 13). The U.S. government even gave Iraq help to develop chemical weapons.[4]

Prior History

When the United States led the invasion of Iraq in 2003, this was not the first time that U.S. and other allied soldiers had gone to war against Saddam Hussein. Back in August 1990, the Iraqi leader had sent armed forces into the neighboring country of Kuwait. This was a small country that had become very wealthy because of its huge reserves of petroleum (oil). Saddam's troops quickly occupied Kuwait, and it became a province (territory) of Iraq.

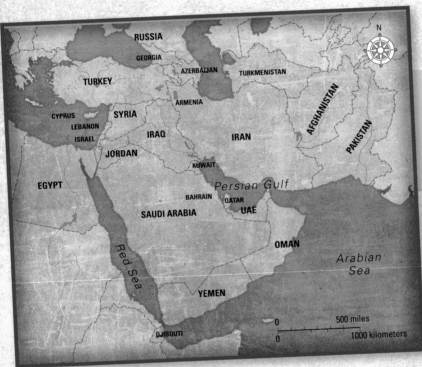

This map shows the location of Iraq and other countries in the Middle East.

The riches of oil

Oil, or petroleum, is one of the most vital and valuable resources in the world. It is used to make a vast variety of fuels, plastics, and important chemicals. Recent figures (from 2010) show that the world consumes over 85 million barrels of oil every day.[2] The Middle East is a major area of oil production. Saudi Arabia alone produces 10 million barrels a day, and Iraq, Iran, and Kuwait produce another 9 million.[3] This means that the Middle East is a hugely important region, especially for industrialized countries such as the United States and many European nations, which have to import huge amounts of oil to meet their needs.

Major world powers, including Russia and the United States, condemned Iraq's invasion of Kuwait. In November 1990, the UN passed a **resolution** demanding that Iraqi forces withdraw from Kuwait by January 15, 1991. If Saddam refused, the UN would give authority to its members to "use all necessary means" to force the Iraqis out.[1] This would mean war.

Operation Desert Storm

The U.S. president at the time was George H. W. Bush, the father of George W. Bush. He began to assemble U.S. forces in Saudi Arabia, a country that was friendly to the United States and bordered both Iraq and Kuwait. Bush also built up an alliance of countries, including the United Kingdom, that would support a war against Saddam. These included many **Arab** and other Islamic nations—a crucial fact because it showed that the United States and United Kingdom were acting with the Muslim world, and not against it. Bush's biggest supporter was the UK prime minister, Margaret Thatcher.

On January 17, 1991, soon after the UN deadline expired, U.S.-led forces attacked Iraq and Kuwait. Most troops were American, with support from Saudi Arabia, the United Kingdom, and Egypt. More than 30 countries took part in the coalition. The operation was called Desert Storm. It was the beginning of what became known as the Gulf War.

In August 1990, King Fahd of Saudi Arabia (right) and President George H.W. Bush (left) agreed on the launch of Operation Desert Shield. U.S. troops were stationed on the Saudi border to prevent a possible Iraqi invasion.

Bombs and missiles struck at Saddam's airfields and military bases. Then, on February 24, ground forces moved into Kuwait.

In three days, they reached the capital, Kuwait City, and much of the Iraqi army had been destroyed. U.S. troops also advanced into Iraq itself, but later withdrew. By February 27, Kuwait had been liberated.

By late February 1991, the United States and its allies were in a very strong position. They could have gone on to conquer Iraq, seize control of the capital city of Baghdad, and overthrow Saddam Hussein. But the coalition armies halted near the Iraqi border. Why did they do this?

There were several reasons. President George H. W. Bush thought some allies would oppose a full-scale invasion of Iraq, and that this might cause the coalition to split up. He also hoped that the Iraqi people would start a rebellion and get rid of Saddam themselves. Other people, such as U.S. Secretary of Defense Dick Cheney, believed an invasion would lead to long-term U.S. involvement in Iraq.

There were two other reasons for halting the invasion. First, the coalition army needed to rest, reorganize, and wait for fresh supplies. Second, U.S. leaders were concerned that TV coverage of further death and destruction in Iraq might turn public opinion against the war.

Decisive words: Bogged down

"If we had gone in there, we would still have forces in Baghdad today. We'd be running the country. We would not have been able to bring everybody home. I think we got it right. We were not going to get bogged down in the problems of trying to take over and govern Iraq."[4]

then-Secretary of Defense Dick Cheney, speaking in 1992

Weapons of mass destruction

Weapons of mass destruction (WMDs) are weapons that can kill or harm large numbers of people and cause major damage to the environment. There are three main types of WMDs:

- *Chemical weapons*: Chemical weapons contain special chemicals that kill humans by attacking the nerves, skin, and other tissues and organs of the body.

- *Biological weapons*: Biological weapons spread bacteria or viruses that cause fatal diseases such as anthrax or smallpox.

- *Nuclear weapons*: Atomic weapons use the process of fission to create an explosion by splitting the nucleus of an atom, which releases a huge amount of energy. Hydrogen bombs create an explosion using the process of fusion.

The search for WMDs

But the main reason for not invading was a resolution made by the Security Council of the UN. This stated that the coalition would not advance further into Iraq if Saddam gave complete and honest details about Iraq's weapons of mass destruction (WMDs). He was told to close down all plants for making these weapons.

The Iraqis had certainly produced and used WMDs in the past. During the 1980s, Saddam had attacked opponents in Iran and his own country with chemical weapons. He had also produced biological weapons and had begun to develop nuclear weapons—although these were never completed.

Now the UN wanted to make certain these terrible weapons had been cleared from Iraq. It sent specially trained inspectors into the country to ensure that all WMDs were destroyed. This turned out to be a difficult and frustrating job, because Saddam refused to cooperate with the inspectors. The suspicion of WMDs was to become a major justification of the invasion of Iraq 12 years later.

The United Nations

The United Nations (UN) was created at the end of World War II, in 1945. Almost every sovereign state (independent country) in the world is a member. The UN's main aims are to encourage global harmony, to uphold human rights, and to help the development of poorer countries. The Security Council of the UN works to maintain international peace and security. It is made up of 15 countries, including 5 permanent members: China, the United States, Russia, the United Kingdom, and France. The other 10 representatives are chosen in rotation from other UN member nations.

Saddam, Terrorism, and 9/11

The Gulf War had ended in an apparent victory for the U.S.-led coalition. Yet, in the years that followed, Iraq was still an independent state, and its leader was still in power. Moreover, Saddam Hussein refused to accept that he had been defeated. In fact, he claimed he had won! In a speech given on July 29, 1991, he told Iraqis: "You are victorious because you have refused humiliation and repression."[1]

Iraq: A divided country

The people of Iraq are made up of a mixture of several **ethnic** and religious groups. There is often unrest between these groups. About 75 percent of the population are Arabs and about 15 percent are Kurds. The major religion is **Islam**: about 62 percent of Muslims belong to the **Shi'a sect**, while the rest are Sunni.[3] Saddam Hussein and his top officials were all Sunnis.

Hiding the evidence

Saddam's defiance angered the Americans and their allies. They hoped he would have been weakened by defeat in the Gulf War, and that opponents in Iraq would have seized control from him or killed him. But this did not happen. Saddam managed to stay in power by killing or **exiling** all rivals and by surrounding himself with very loyal members of his own family or tribe.

Saddam's behavior over WMDs made the Americans and the UN even angrier. At first, he claimed to be destroying these weapons—before UN inspectors arrived.[2] This gave him the chance to get rid of some items before anyone knew about them. Then, Saddam organized a secret program of concealing weapon sites and hiding important documents about them.

When the UN weapons inspectors started their work in 1991, Iraqi officials were not helpful. Most denied that WMDs existed or refused to provide information. Others prevented the inspectors from visiting certain sites. Nevertheless, chemical weapons were found, in addition to evidence of a program to develop nuclear warheads.

A new doctrine

President George H. W. Bush, who had helped begin the Gulf War, was a Republican who represented conservative ideas. After the Gulf War, some of his close advisers (from a group of Republicans known as **neoconservatives**, or "neocons" for short) now developed an idea for dealing with dangerous foreign leaders like Saddam. They believed that the United States should strike first to get rid of these leaders and establish a safer government in these countries. This **doctrine** was called "**regime** change."

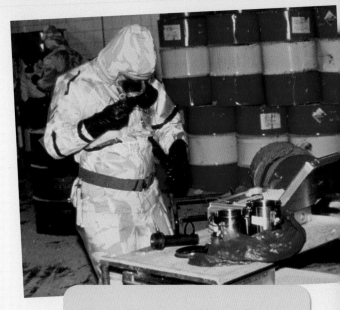

After the liberation of Kuwait, United Nations inspectors entered Iraq to search for evidence of WMDs (weapons of mass destruction).

Who were the leading neocons in government?

The following are some of the leading U.S. conservative politicians who had great influence during the presidencies of George H. W. Bush and his son George W. Bush:

- Dick Cheney, secretary of defense (1989–1993) and vice president (2001–2009)

- Paul Wolfowitz, official in the State Department and Department of Defense

- Donald Rumsfeld, secretary of defense (1975–1977 and 2001–2006)

- Richard Perle, political adviser to many Republican presidents.

But in January 1993, the United States elected a new president—Bill Clinton. He was a Democrat who represented the more liberal side of U.S. politics, and so the neocons no longer had any direct influence on government policy. Clinton disagreed with their ideas of **preemptive** (first) strikes and regime change in hostile countries. He preferred to take military action abroad in alliance with other countries.

The rise of terrorism

Meanwhile, another and much bigger threat to world peace was growing in strength. Small bands of Muslims were inspired by the teachings and ideals of Islamic fundamentalism. They began violent terrorist campaigns against people they believed were hostile to Islam. The violence included suicide bombings, **assassinations**, and armed attacks on **civilians**.

What is Islamic fundamentalism?

The "fundamentals" of a subject are its foundations or basic beliefs. **Fundamentalist** Muslims want a return to the core ideas of Islam, based entirely on their own strict interpretation of the words of the Quran (the central religious text of Islam) and other teachings of the Prophet Muhammad. Some fundamentalists have been prepared to use extreme violence (including terrorism) to force their beliefs on other people. Their eventual aim has been to make the whole world an Islamic state under the rule of *sharia* (the moral and religious laws outlined by the Prophet). They believe that nonbelievers deserve to be killed. The vast majority of Muslims disagree with these views, which they see as a perversion (extreme misinterpretation) of Muhammad's teachings.

One of the main targets of terrorist rage was the United States. It was seen as an imperialist power (a country that aggressively extends its rule) that had killed or harmed Muslims in the Middle East in conflicts such as the Gulf War. The United States was also the most powerful supporter of Israel, which had been founded in 1948. Many Muslims were angry about the Israelis' treatment of the Palestinian people. **Extremists** wished to see Israel destroyed.

Israel and the Palestinians

Israel was founded after World War II as a homeland for the Jewish people. Many native Palestinians were forced to move to make room for the new state. This created much hostility among neighboring Arab countries, which have since made several attempts to invade or take control of Israeli territory. But Israel has survived, largely thanks to massive economic and military support from the United States, and it has seized more land from the Palestinians. Many leaders have attempted to find a settlement to the conflict between Israelis and Palestinians, but none has succeeded. Israel is a major issue in relations between the United States and the Muslim world.

Blindfolded American hostages, seized during the occupation of the U.S. Embassy in Tehran in 1979, were paraded by their militant Iranian captors.

Striking at the United States

Back in the late 1970s and early 1980s, there had been increased hostility between some Muslim countries and the United States. In 1979, the people of Iran overthrew the shah (a monarch like a king) and his government and turned their country into an Islamic **republic**. Extremists took over the U.S. **embassy** in Teheran and took 66 Americans hostage. A U.S. military rescue mission failed, and the hostages were not released until 1981. This was a major reason why Western nations were willing to give support to Iraq in its war with Iran (see page 5).

The Iran hostage crisis damaged relations between the United States and parts of the Middle East. There were more terrorist incidents. In October 1981, fundamentalists assassinated President Anwar Sadat of Egypt because of his support for Israel and the United States. In 1983, the U.S. embassy in Beirut, Lebanon, was bombed. In 1989, there was a suicide attack in Tel Aviv, Israel.

Then, in the 1990s, the number of Islamic terrorist attacks around the world increased. Among these was the first bombing of the World Trade Center in New York, which killed six people in 1993. In 1994, another bomb killed 85 Jewish people in Buenos Aires, Argentina. In 1996, 20 people died in an attack on a housing complex in Khobar, Saudi Arabia.

Iraq and extremism

Was Saddam Hussein involved with the terrorists? Many countries in the UN believed he was, but they had no proof. However, the growth of **Islamist** terrorism certainly helped the Iraqi dictator to stay in power. Extremists saw him as a hero of Islam who had defied the might of the U.S. armed forces and survived after the U.S. invasion of 1991.

Saddam played up to this by strengthening his image as a devout (deeply religious) Muslim—despite the fact that much of his violence had been aimed at other Muslims. He financed the building of several new **mosques** in Baghdad and increased religious teachings in schools. He even produced a special copy of the Quran, which he claimed had been written with his own blood.[4]

All this, of course, made him a bigger threat than ever. The U.S. government already knew that Iraq had possessed chemical weapons and had developed biological weapons and a nuclear weapons program. It also knew that Saddam was running a savage and repressive regime and using torture and other violence to suppress his opponents at home.

Plotting regime change

In 1996, U.S. neocon officials began drawing up a wide-ranging plan to change the political balance of the Middle East. For example, the group (led by Richard Perle) wrote a report for the government of Israel. This recommended that the United States

Tony Blair

Born: Edinburgh, Scotland, 1953

Role: UK prime minister, 1997–2007

Born in Scotland, Tony Blair trained as a barrister (a high-ranking lawyer) and became a member of **Parliament** in 1983. He was elected as head of the Labour Party in 1994, after the sudden death of the previous leader, John Smith. Blair played a major role in the reshaping of his party, with policies that were called "New Labour." Many people thought that New Labour signaled a move away from traditional socialist values, giving less influence to the trade unions, forging better links with industry, and pledging not to raise taxes. The party's new style appealed to voters, and in 1997, Labour was elected to government with a huge majority. Blair became the UK prime minister.

and Israel should abandon all peace negotiations in the Middle East. Instead, the Israelis should launch surprise attacks on hostile countries—including Iraq.

The report recommended that the Israelis should "focus on removing Saddam Hussein from power in Iraq."[5] It even suggested a complex plot for assassinating him. Israeli leaders rejected the report, but Perle and his colleagues would later revive many of their ideas during the presidency of George W. Bush, five years later.

The rise of Tony Blair

Meanwhile, a new leader had emerged in the United Kingdom. Tony Blair was elected as British prime minister on May 2, 1997. He would later become the firmest supporter of U.S. policy in Iraq and Afghanistan. Blair came to share many of the beliefs about regime change and preemptive action that were developed by the neocons and George W. Bush.

At first glance, this was a surprising alliance. Bush and the neocons were Republicans, who are traditionally conservative and nationalistic. Blair and his cabinet belonged to the UK Labour Party, which was traditionally an agent of reform, high taxation, and liberal foreign policy. Yet the warm friendship between the two young leaders would lead to a significant strengthening of the historic "special relationship" between the United States and the United Kingdom.

Tony Blair led the UK Labour Party to an overwhelming victory in the 1997 election. At 43, he became the youngest British prime minister for nearly two centuries.

Al-Qaeda and Saddam

In 1998, Islamist terrorists began to focus their attacks more directly at the United States. That August, there were simultaneous bombings of U.S. embassies in two East African cities—Nairobi and Dar es Salaam. More than 301 people were killed, and over 5,000 were injured.[6] These acts of terror were the work of the extremist organization **al-Qaeda.**

Al-Qaeda

Al-Qaeda (Arabic for "the foundation") is an Islamic terrorist organization. It was founded in Pakistan in about 1988 by a group of radical Muslims that included Osama bin Laden, a wealthy Saudi Arab.[9] Al-Qaeda's first aim was to unite all extremist Islamic groups under its leadership. Together, they would fight a *jihad* (holy struggle) to enforce *sharia* law throughout the Muslim world. Since then, units of al-Qaeda in many countries have carried out terrorist attacks against civilians and military personnel.

Osama bin Laden (center) and other *jihadists* learned military skills during the fighting against Soviet forces in Afghanistan during the 1980s.

Meanwhile, tension was rising over Iraq. The U.S. government felt that Saddam was not fully cooperating with weapons inspections and was breaking the terms of the cease-fire. It struck back with "Operation Desert Fox" in December. U.S. and UK forces bombed Iraq for four days, aiming to destroy weapons-making sites. Over 1,200 Iraqis died.[7]

9/11

In January 2001, George W. Bush succeeded Bill Clinton as president. Bush was a conservative Republican, and he reappointed many of the officials who had served his father. At his **inauguration**, the new president said, "We will confront weapons of mass destruction, so that a new century is spared new horrors."[8]

But it was an entirely unexpected "weapon of mass destruction" that reshaped Bush's presidency and changed the course of history. On September 11, 2001 (also called 9/11), terrorists hijacked (forcibly took over) four airliners on flights across the United States. They deliberately flew two planes into the World Trade Center in New York. A third plane hit the Pentagon in Washington, D.C., the home of the U.S. Department of Defense, while the fourth crashed in a field in Pennsylvania.

The World Trade Center was destroyed, and nearly 3,000 people died in the attacks. It was soon clear that the attacks had been plotted and carried out by terrorists belonging to al-Qaeda. The group's leader, Osama bin Laden, at first denied that his organization was responsible for the attacks, but he later claimed he had helped to plan them.

George W. Bush

Born: New Haven, Connecticut, 1946

Role: 43rd U.S. president, 2001–2009

George W. Bush was the eldest son of another U.S. president, George H. W. Bush. He worked in the oil industry before being elected governor of Texas in 1994. After a very close contest against Democratic candidate Al Gore, Bush was elected president in 2000. Among his first acts were to announce huge tax cuts, to build up better trade links with Latin America, and to withdraw support for an international agreement on climate change. The horrific events of 9/11 caused him to change his agenda, which led to the controversial wars in Afghanistan and Iraq. Bush was later re-elected for a second term in 2004.

The Road to War

The horror of the 9/11 attacks stunned the world. Many governments condemned the attacks and sent messages of sympathy and support to President Bush. Among the first leaders to contact him was UK Prime Minister Tony Blair. This created a special bond between the two men. "The conversation helped cement the closest friendship I would form with any foreign leader," Bush later wrote.[1]

Who was behind 9/11?

The United States was the strongest nation on the planet. Yet somehow a small band of extremists had gotten through its defenses to carry out a major act of violence on U.S. soil. The attack was not just tragic—it was humiliating. President Bush and his administration felt they had to hit back at the terrorists quickly and effectively.

First, there were important questions to answer. Where had the hijackers come from? Who had trained them? Who had planned the assault? The **Federal Bureau of Investigation (FBI)** and U.S. **intelligence** agencies immediately began investigations. It soon seemed clear that the terrorists had been members of al-Qaeda, and that they had followed a plan organized by Osama bin Laden, who was based in Afghanistan.

Donald H. Rumsfeld

Born: Evanston, Illinois, 1932

Role: U.S. secretary of defense, 1975–1977 and 2001–2006

Donald Rumsfeld was elected as a congressman in 1962, at the age of only 30. He held a government job under President Richard Nixon in 1969, and went on to serve many other Republican presidents. He was appointed chief of staff by President Gerald Ford in 1974, and he became secretary of defense a year later. After a period in business, Rumsfeld became secretary of defense again when George W. Bush appointed him in 2001.

Did you know? Rumsfeld has been both the youngest and the oldest secretary of defense in U.S. history.

Blaming Saddam

Even so, members of the Bush administration were convinced that Saddam Hussein was somehow behind the plot. Some believed this might be a good excuse to attack Iraq again. This was clearly shown by a note written by an aide to Secretary of Defense Donald Rumsfeld on September 11. The note recorded the words of Rumsfeld at a meeting that day: "Judge whether good enough hit S.H. [Saddam Hussein]. Go massive. Sweep it all up."[2]

Decisive words: Launching the war

"Our enemy is a radical network of terrorists and every government that supports them. Our war on terror begins with al-Qaeda, but it does not end there. It will not end until every terrorist group of global reach has been found, stopped, and defeated... We will pursue nations that provide aid or safe haven to terrorism. Every nation in every region now has a decision to make: Either you are with us or you are with the terrorists."

George W. Bush, speaking to Congress and the nation, September 20, 2001[4]

President Bush was also anxious to pin the blame on Iraq. The day after the attacks, Bush talked to Richard Clarke, his chief adviser on counterterrorism (fighting terrorism), telling him: "See if Saddam did this. See if he's linked in any way." Clarke replied that it was the work of al-Qaeda, and no link with Iraq had been found. Nonetheless, Bush said, "Look into Iraq, Saddam."[3]

George W. Bush (right) and Secretary of Defense Donald Rumsfeld (left) visited the Pentagon the day after the 9/11 terrorist attacks to inspect the damage.

19

The invasion of Afghanistan

The U.S. **Congress** quickly voted to give the president powers to use military force against the people responsible for the 9/11 attacks. Bush and his officials had by now concluded that Osama bin Laden and al-Qaeda were to blame. Therefore, on October 7, a moderately sized U.S. force (supported by Afghan fighters opposed to the **Taliban** government as well as UK and Australian troops) launched the first of its strikes in Afghanistan. A new war had begun.

The main target of the invasion was to capture bin Laden and other terrorist leaders and destroy al-Qaeda. But the U.S.-led forces also aimed to overthrow the country's rulers, the Taliban. This militant Islamist group had seized power in 1996 and had given a safe haven to anti-Western terrorists, including al-Qaeda. In mid-November 2001, the Taliban leaders had fled from Kabul, the Afghan capital. Many went into hiding over the border in Pakistan.

Losing bin Laden

After 9/11, the FBI offered a reward of up to $25 million for information leading to the capture or death of Osama bin Laden.[8] Despite this, U.S. forces failed to find the al-Qaeda leader during the 2001 Afghanistan invasion. From December 12 to 17, 2001, special troops surrounded a system of caves in the Tora Bora mountains, believing bin Laden was in hiding there. But he was not found. Some experts think he slipped away during the battle and took refuge in Pakistan.

Anti-Taliban Afghan fighters watch from a distance as U.S. forces bomb the Tora Bora mountains.

By early December, the U.S.-led invaders had taken control of most of the country. Afghanistan became an Islamic republic, and democratic elections were planned. More than 770 suspected terrorists seized during the invasion were sent to a special U.S. prison at Guantánamo Bay in Cuba, some based on almost no evidence.[5] Bush's first venture in regime change looked like it would be a success.

"Axis of evil"

The conquest of Afghanistan was only the start of what President Bush had called "our war on terror." There were many other possible targets. The **Central Intelligence Agency (CIA)** and other U.S. intelligence bodies reported that as many as 50 other countries were giving shelter to al-Qaeda around the world.[6] Among them was Iraq.

President Bush gave the annual State of the Union address to the nation on January 29, 2002. He stated that tens of thousands of trained terrorists were still at large globally and had to be pursued. He singled out North Korea, Iran, and Iraq as posing the biggest threats, saying: "States like these, and their terrorist allies, constitute an axis of evil, arming to threaten the peace of the world."[7]

The CIA

The CIA gathers information about other countries. It collects and evaluates facts about politics, economics, military forces, and other important topics and passes them on to other U.S. government agencies. The CIA also acts to protect the country's security. This includes monitoring the activities of hostile nations and combatting the work of foreign spies. The agency has also been accused of spying on U.S. citizens.

Bush and Blair

By this time, George W. Bush and Tony Blair had become good friends. During 2002, the UK leader visited the United States several times and stayed with his family at Bush's home in Crawford, Texas, and at the White House. Bush and his family had been guests at Blair's official home, Chequers.

As previously mentioned (see page 15), the alliance between the two seemed surprising, given their different political backgrounds. But, in fact, they had many points in common. Both had secure and privileged backgrounds, and both believed in less state control over many aspects of life. More significantly, both had strong Christian beliefs, which influenced many of their decisions.

Tony Blair made several visits to the U.S. during 2002, often hosted by George and Laura Bush (center). The Bush and Blair families became very close.

Above all, they were both determined to get rid of Saddam Hussein, whom they considered a threat to world peace. The pair was also planning what would happen after that. Bush wrote later: "Tony and I would have an obligation to help the Iraqi people replace Saddam's tyranny [a government in which a single person has total power] with a democracy."[9] Blair expressed something similar when he said, "I still believe that leaving Saddam in power was a bigger risk to our security than removing him."[10]

Searching for evidence of WMDs

Both the U.S. and UK administrations made repeated warnings about Iraq and called for rapid and decisive action. U.S. Vice President Dick Cheney told a television interviewer that he was "almost certain" of further terrorist attacks on the United States.[11] Bush and Blair now wanted to make a strong case for going to war with Saddam, by proving that he posed a major threat.

To do this, they had to find evidence that Saddam was still hiding or producing WMDs. The CIA and other agencies were urged to produce it quickly. But nothing definite was discovered, and the urgency of the quest often led to claims that were misleading or mistaken.

Decisive words: "Saddam needs to go"

"I made up my mind that Saddam needs to go. The policy of my government is that he goes."

George W. Bush, speaking to ITV interviewer Trevor McDonald, April 6, 2002[14]

For example, in February 2002, the CIA received reports that Iraq was trying to buy "yellowcake" (a form of concentrated uranium used to create nuclear reactions) from the African state of Niger. If this were true, it would show that Saddam was developing nuclear weapons. A U.S. official was sent to investigate and told the CIA the report was wrong. Despite this, Bush continued to claim it was true.[12]

Decisive words: Striking first

In the summer of 2002, President Bush gave signals that he was already committed to the doctrine of regime change. On June 1, 2002, he showed he was also in favor of "preemptive action." In a speech to military cadets, he said:

"We cannot defend America and our friends by hoping for the best... The war on terror will not be won on the defensive. We must take the battle to the enemy, disrupt his plans, and confront the worst threats before they emerge. The only path to safety is the path of action. And this nation will act... Our security will require all Americans to be ready for preemptive action when necessary to defend our liberty and to defend our lives."[13]

23

Decision Time

By July 2002, war with Iraq was inevitable. It is possible that President Bush had already made the decision to remove Saddam from power, even if he had not announced it. He had mentioned it in private conversations. He had ordered U.S. military chiefs, headed by General Tommy Franks, to draw up a detailed plan for the invasion. Two things were still to be decided—how to justify the attack to the rest of the world, and what to do with Iraq once the war was over.

Secrets in Downing Street

Tony Blair was surprised at how fast things were moving. In his talks with Bush, he had argued that invasion should be their last resort. He wanted to wait until there was a clear UN resolution on Iraq, and until Saddam had ignored it. They could only invade, he wrote, "on the basis of non-compliance [failure to obey] with UN resolutions."[1] However, some UK officials believed the United States was not bothered by Blair's conditions.[2] The U.S. government was working on a definite timetable for war.

So, on July 23, Blair held a secret (and urgent) meeting at 10 Downing Street, the headquarters of the UK government, with close colleagues and intelligence chiefs. A record of this meeting

President Bush and senior officials in his administration, including Vice President Dick Cheney (to Bush's right), Secretary of State Condoleezza Rice and ex-Secretary of State Colin Powell (both to Bush's left) met regularly in the White House to oversee progress in Iraq.

was made, and it shows that Blair wanted a fuller picture of U.S. planning before making a firm decision. But the memo later states: "It seemed clear that Bush had already made up his mind to take military action."[3]

Debates in the White House

Meanwhile, the Bush administration was moving ahead with definite plans for the attack. On August 5, General Franks showed the president his detailed day-by-day schedule for the Iraq invasion. Bush was satisfied: "I like the concept," he said.[4]

Rumsfeld and Cheney were now pushing hard for swift action against Saddam. But Secretary of State Colin Powell—like Blair—wanted more caution. He argued that the United States should not invade without the full backing of the UN. He also told Bush that regime change would leave the United States in charge of governing 25 million Iraqis, and that planning for this was being neglected.[5] This problem had been deliberately avoided by the cautious policy used in the first Gulf War.

Dick Cheney

Born: Lincoln, Nebraska, 1941

Role: U.S. vice president, 2001–2009

Dick Cheney grew up in a small town in rural Wyoming. He began his political career in the Wyoming Senate, before being hired as a White House aide and becoming President Gerald Ford's chief of staff in 1976. Cheney was elected six times to the House of Representatives. He served as George H. W. Bush's secretary of defense, during which time he was in charge of Operation Desert Storm. In 2000, Cheney became vice president to George W. Bush, and he campaigned strongly for the invasion of Iraq.

But in many ways, it was too late. A kind of invasion had already started, without the agreement of the UN. Special CIA teams were in place in Iraq. They contacted and organized local liberation groups hostile to Saddam, such as the Kurdish *peshmerga* (fighters for an independent Kurdish state). They also gathered information about invasion routes and the locations of key Iraqi officials. At the same time, there was an increase in air strikes by U.S. and UK warplanes and missiles, aimed at crippling Iraqi air defense systems.

Bending the evidence

Bush and Blair met again at the president's country retreat of Camp David, in Maryland, on September 7. Blair was pleased to hear Bush had decided to wait for a UN resolution, which would demand that Saddam allow weapons inspectors back into Iraq.[6] But at a press conference that day, President Bush said bluntly, "Saddam Hussein possesses weapons of mass destruction."[7]

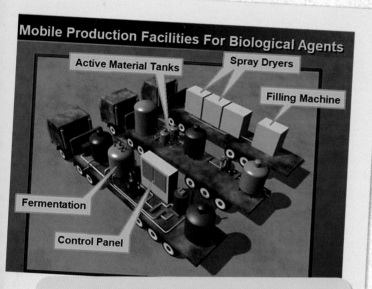

This image—created using intelligence that was later proved unreliable—illustrates Iraqi mobile units for manufacturing WMDs. Secretary of State Colin Powell showed this to the UN Security Council as part of the Bush administration's argument against Iraq.

How could Bush know this for certain? There had been no weapons inspections in Iraq for nearly four years. Most of the information was coming from U.S. intelligence agencies, and this information was often unreliable. This was partly because many of the sources of information were anxious to encourage an invasion for their own political benefit. But, as previously mentioned, the Bush administration tended to ignore data that did not back up its case for war and to use misleading stories as evidence to show that Saddam had WMDs.

Here are three more examples of misleading stories and facts:

- *The Iraqi defector.* In August 2002, Vice President Cheney stated that Iraq was actively developing nuclear weapons. He claimed that the evidence came from Saddam's son-in-law, who defected from Iraq in 1995. But, in fact, the **defector** had said the opposite—that Saddam had done no work on nuclear weapons since 1991.[8]

- *The aluminum tubes*: In September 2002, senior Bush officials said that Iraq was buying aluminum tubes. They claimed that these would be used for enriching uranium for nuclear weapons—ignoring the advice of nuclear experts that they could not be used for that purpose.[9]

- *"Curveball"*: Another Iraqi defector was given the code name "Curveball." He claimed to have worked on building mobile laboratories for making biological weapons. Interrogators (people who question suspects) warned that he was lying, but the Bush team still used his claims as evidence in the invasion buildup.[10]

Two important resolutions

Next came another big step toward war. On October 11, 2002, Congress voted on a resolution authorizing the use of U.S. armed forces against Iraq. It was passed with a large majority. This meant that regime change in Iraq was now part of the official policy of the U.S. government. There was a legal basis (in the United States, if not internationally) that allowed the president to order the invasion.

On November 8, the UN Security Council passed an even more important resolution. This was Resolution 1441, which Bush had been eagerly waiting for. It stated that Saddam had broken the terms of a previous resolution about WMDs and must immediately start to cooperate with UN inspectors. Within a month, Saddam had invited the inspectors back into Iraq.

Decisive words: Taking out Saddam

"At some point we will conclude that enough is enough and take him [Saddam] out. He's a liar and he's got no intention of disarming... If the decision is made [by the United States] to go to war, we'll go back to the Security Council. We won't ask for permission, we shall ask for support."

George W. Bush, talking with Spain's president, José María Aznar, December 18, 2002[11]

Blix draws a blank

By Christmas 2002, President Bush was growing very impatient. The team of UN weapons inspectors, led by Hans Blix, was at work in Iraq, but it had not found any evidence of WMDs. More importantly, Blix believed that within a few months his team would be able to prove that Saddam had disarmed. But Bush felt they were not trying hard enough, and he put intense pressure on the team. Blix said later, "I think they had a set mind. The Americans needed WMD[s] to justify the Iraq War."[12]

President Bush hosted Blair at the White House again on January 31, 2003. Blair said they needed a second UN resolution—one that made it clear that an invasion of Iraq was the only answer. (Resolution 1441 had not done this.) Many British people were opposed to the war, and Blair might lose the support of his own political party without a second resolution. Bush reluctantly agreed to wait.

Failure at the UN

The Bush administration put a huge amount of effort into persuading the UN Security Council to pass a second resolution.

On February 15, 2003, as many as 10 million people worldwide took part in demonstrations against the looming Iraq War. It was one of the biggest global protests ever—but the invasion still went ahead.

On February 5, Colin Powell gave a speech to the 15 council members. He made many claims about the Iraqi threat. These included a strong connection between Iraq and al-Qaeda, the existence of mobile WMD units, and the Iraqi production of cultures of anthrax (a deadly disease). Most of these claims were later proven to be false.

On February 24, the United States, the United Kingdom, and Spain proposed the resolution on Iraq. But most members of the Security Council declared they would not vote at all. They were opposed to what they saw as unjustified regime change, and they believed there was no long-term benefit to getting rid of Saddam. Besides this, the weapons inspectors were about to conclude that there were no WMDs in Iraq.

The resolution could not be passed, so it was withdrawn. Many authorities were certain that the invasion would be illegal under international law.

The "dodgy dossier"

In the summer of 2002, Blair had asked for a "dossier," or collection of documents, to be compiled. It would be given to journalists and offer an explanation of the reasons for invading Iraq. The first version was published soon afterward and contained the claim that the Iraqis could deploy chemical or biological weapons within 45 minutes of an invasion. This was later proven to be incorrect. The second dossier, on February 3, 2003, soon came to be known as the "dodgy [unreliable] dossier." This was mainly because some of the information was based on unnamed or unreliable sources, which were also proven wrong.

Time runs out

But President Bush appeared determined to invade Iraq—even without allies or approval. Blair remained a loyal supporter, promising, "I'm there to the very end."[13] So, on March 17, Bush gave Saddam Hussein an ultimatum (final statement of terms): leave within 48 hours or we invade. U.S. armed forces were already in place in Kuwait.

There was one last hurdle. Blair had to get approval for the war from the UK Parliament. On March 18, he made an impassioned speech to the House of Commons. He argued that force was the only answer to Saddam, saying: "The only persuasive power to which he responds is 250,000 allied troops on his doorstep."[14] The House of Commons voted for war, by 412 to 149.[15]

Shock and Awe

On March 18, members of the UK Parliament had voted in favor of the Iraq War. But by that time, the war was already under way. Some U.S. troops had entered the Kurdish region in northern Iraq. Special forces were destroying Iraqi missile launchpads. U.S. and UK aircraft were bombing key sites in Baghdad and elsewhere.

Trying for a knockout

President Bush's time limit for Saddam ran out on March 19, 2003. The Iraqi leader had made no move to leave his country. Indeed, U.S. intelligence reports claimed he was visiting his sons and daughters at Dora Farm, near Baghdad. Early that morning, Bush made his first major decision of the war. He gave orders for an air attack on the farm, in an attempt to kill Saddam. This could have ended the war before it had started.

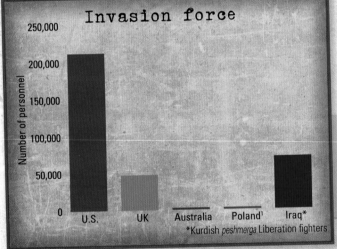

Invasion force

Number of personnel: 250,000 / 200,000 / 150,000 / 100,000 / 50,000 / 0

U.S.   UK   Australia   Poland[1]   Iraq*
*Kurdish *peshmerga* Liberation fighters

The U.S.-led force that invaded Iraq consisted mostly of personnel from five countries.

From the Oval Office of the White House, Bush made sure all his military and intelligence commanders were ready. Then, he simply said, "Let's go."[2] U.S. combat aircraft dropped four powerful bombs on the compound at Dora Farm, while U.S. warships launched missiles at the same site. The attack killed 15 Iraqis, but Saddam was not in the compound. The intelligence report had been wrong.

Decisive words: Shaping world history

"I kind of think that the decisions taken in the next few weeks will determine the rest of the world for years to come. As primary players we have the chance to shape the issues."

Tony Blair, talking by telephone with George W. Bush, March 20, 2003[3]

The invasion begins

The major part of the invasion began the next morning. The number of U.S. and UK air strikes increased, in a display of power intended to "shock and awe" the Iraqis. Baghdad was the first target, receiving a massive bombardment that lasted two days. The mission's aim was to kill members of the Iraqi leadership and destroy communications posts. Missiles and bombs hit Saddam's palaces, the Foreign Ministry, and other important buildings.

Meanwhile, land forces also went into action. One body of U.S. and UK ground troops crossed over the border from Kuwait. By March 21, it had advanced over 100 miles (160 kilometers) into southern Iraq. Other troops landed by sea on the coast south of Baghdad and seized control of important ports and oilfields. The bigger U.S. forces drove in a two-pronged attack toward Baghdad, while the smaller British Army forces advanced toward Basra.

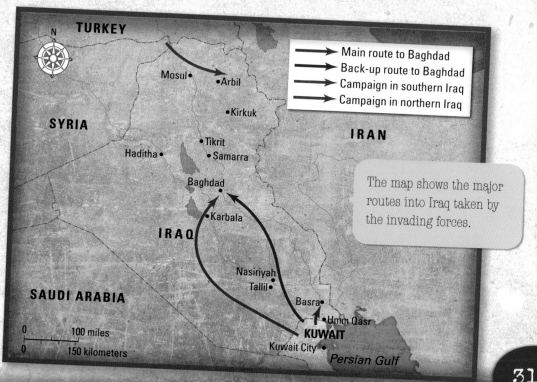

The map shows the major routes into Iraq taken by the invading forces.

The Iraqi forces were demoralized and poorly armed. That evening, President Bush proudly reported to Blair that the coalition was not bothering to take prisoners, because the Iraqis were happy to take off their uniforms and simply run away.[4] They did this even though Saddam had promised a reward of over $30,000 to anyone who captured a U.S. soldier.[5]

The first week of the invasion had brought rapid success for the U.S. coalition forces. But during the second week, progress slowed down. Troops found it hard to get through the desert, where they faced high winds, sand storms, and searing heat. There was tougher resistance from **militia** soldiers, such as the *fedayeen* (irregular forces fiercely loyal to Saddam), led by Saddam's son Uday. Iraqis also set fire to over 30 oil wells, and these fires had to be put out.

Allies in debate

Bush and Blair did not always agree—at first. In his autobiography, Blair describes how he wanted the invasion coalition to seek UN support for reconstructing Iraq after the war, even if the UN had not supported the invasion before. On March 27, he contacted Bush. According to Blair:

> My aim was to persuade the U.S. that as soon as the fighting stopped, the whole political process should be put under the UN... The Americans' belief was that the UN got in the way... It was a hard sell with George [Bush], and even harder with Dick [Cheney]. But in the end we got agreement that the UN should come in.[7]

At this point, the operation of the war was in the hands of the armed forces and the commanders. Bush and Blair had few decisions to make. They could only watch the progress and give encouragement to their staff and allies. On April 2, Bush told Australian Prime Minister John Howard, "Saddam has his fingers around the throat of the Iraqi people, and he has two fingers left and we are prying them loose."[6]

Into Baghdad

By early April, things were moving more quickly again. The leading part of the U.S. land forces was just 10 miles (16 kilometers) from Baghdad. UK troops were nearing Iraq's second major city, Basra. U.S. paratroopers had landed in the north of the country, where they joined up with CIA units and bands of Iraqi *peshmerga* fighters, and they advanced on the town of Kirkuk.

On April 5, U.S. forces began an attack on Baghdad. After fierce fighting, they captured one of Saddam's main palaces and crossed the Tigris River to reach the city center. The invaders took control of central Baghdad on April 9. Saddam had vanished, and other Iraqi leaders had surrendered or run away.

Saddam's long reign as dictator of Iraq was over. Later that day, his fall was symbolized when U.S. soldiers used an armored vehicle to pull down a 40-foot- (12-meter-) tall statue of the Iraqi leader. A crowd of Iraqis celebrated by smashing the statue and jumping on it. Images of this moment were seen all over the world.

All the same, President Bush remained cautious when he heard the news. "The strategy is paying off," he said to Spain's prime minister, José María Aznar. "You won't see us doing any victory dances."[8] Aznar had been a strong supporter of U.S. action against Saddam.

For the Iraq invasion, the U.S. military issued troops with a complete deck of playing cards, which showed the faces and names of the most wanted men of Saddam's regime. Saddam himself was the Ace of Spades.

Taking control

The capture of Baghdad did not mark the end of the invasion. In other parts of Iraq, coalition troops were still fighting. UK forces had seized control of Basra and were now moving north to join U.S. forces attacking the town of Amarah. In the north, the Kurdish militias, aided by special U.S. units, were driving back Iraqi troops outside Kirkuk. Tikrit, in central Iraq, fell on April 15.

The collapse of Saddam's regime left the country without a government or leader. In the anarchy (lawlessness) that followed, old hostilities flared up between tribes, regions, and cities. **Civil war** seemed to be taking over. The invading armies had to move quickly, in an attempt to impose order in several areas.

"Mission accomplished"

President Bush had promised no "victory dances." Yet on May 1, he arrived by jet combat aircraft on the flight deck of the carrier USS *Abraham Lincoln*. The ship was off the California coast, having just returned from action in the Middle East. Still wearing his flight suit, Bush announced to the world that major combat operations in Iraq had ended, and that the United States had prevailed.

This was a victory speech— though not a dance. Behind Bush hung a giant banner reading: "MISSION ACCOMPLISHED." But many people saw the banner and the president's triumphant speech as mistaken. The invasion was over, but Iraq was in chaos. Many Iraqis had been killed or wounded during the war, and this caused growing fear and resentment. Nobody knew exactly where the WMDs were located, or if they actually existed. Surely the mission had only just started?

Decisive words: Bush claims victory

"In this battle, we have fought for the cause of liberty, and for the peace of the world… The transition from dictatorship to democracy will take time, but it is worth every effort. Our coalition will stay until our work is done. Then we will leave, and we will leave behind a free Iraq... The liberation of Iraq is a crucial advance in the campaign against terror."

George W. Bush, speaking aboard the USS Abraham Lincoln, *May 1, 2003*[9]

But was it a mistake? Some government officials later claimed that the banner belonged to the ship and merely stated that its mission was accomplished–in which case it was certainly a mistake for Bush to stand in front of it when he made his speech. However, just over a month later, on June 6, the president repeated his message when he spoke to resting US troops in Qatar. He said: "America sent you on a mission to remove a grave threat and to liberate an oppressed people, and that mission has been accomplished." [10]

Death count

There are many disagreements over figures for **casualties**, even from reliable sources. The true totals, especially for those of Iraqi civilian deaths, may never be known. The following reflects estimates of the numbers of people killed during the Iraq invasion, from March 19 to May 1, 2003:

Group affected	Total number of casualties
Coalition forces	
United States	139
United Kingdom	33[11]
Iraqi	
Military personnel	7,600–10,800[12]
Civilians	7,299[13]

The U.S. and British air attacks on Iraq caused a huge amount of death and damage. This photo shows the remains of a house in Baghdad after a coalition bomb strike.

The Bloody Years

The invasion of Iraq had been a triumph. U.S.-led forces had achieved their objectives swiftly and efficiently, and with very small losses on their own side. Now the difficult part of the operation began: rebuilding a shattered, divided, and leaderless country. Had Bush, Blair, and their teams planned thoroughly enough for the aftermath of war?

No quick fix

In fact, the U.S. Department of Defense had come up with a postwar plan. It wanted to install a new leader in Baghdad—an Iraqi exile named Ahmed Chalabi. Chalabi was an opponent of Saddam who had been living in the United States. Under the Department of Defense plan he would become president and appoint other exiled politicians to form a new government. This might allow the coalition forces to exit Iraq very quickly.

But President Bush said that he did not want to select the new rulers. He felt that the Iraqi people, not Washington, D.C., should choose the new government of Iraq.[1] The U.S. government had established the Iraqi people's freedom, and now it wanted to establish democratic rule with elections. So, Bush rejected the Department of Defense's plan. Unfortunately, many believed there was not an adequate plan to replace it.

Ex-soldiers from the disbanded Iraqi army staged angry and violent protests in Basra in January 2004. British troops moved in to control them.

Many coalition soldiers were killed or wounded by improvised explosive devices (IEDs) planted by insurgents next to roads and tracks.

When the invasion was complete, President Bush made his next crucial decision. He appointed Paul Bremer to head the provisional (temporary) authority that would govern and rebuild Iraq. Bremer was an experienced diplomat (an official representing a country abroad) who had served in many countries.

One of Bremer's first acts, on May 16, was to disband the Iraqi army and the Iraqi Defense Ministry. He also dissolved the police force, removed members of Saddam's Ba'ath Party from government posts, and dismissed many teachers and other civil servants who had connections with the Ba'athists.

These were disastrous moves. For a start, up to 400,000 soldiers were put out of work, leaving them angry and poor.[2] The ex-soldiers had weapons they were trained to use, and many later joined the insurgency against U.S. occupying forces. The measure deprived the government of a vast number of skilled and experienced officials who were needed for the efficient running of the country. It also destroyed most of the country's security system, meaning that normal life could not continue on safely.

As a result, the first Iraqi insurgency (revolt) began soon afterward with a wave of daily actions against U.S. and UK troops by Sunnis. The attackers were mostly small groups of guerrillas (soldiers fighting against regular armies) or bombers. They left **improvised explosive devices (IEDs)** on roads or in buildings, where they could be detonated (set off) to kill patrolling soldiers. Most attacks took place in the "Sunni Triangle," an area north of Baghdad.

The violence grows

The coalition armies were succeeding in eliminating the important figures of Saddam's regime. On July 22, the dictator's sons, Uday and Qusay, were killed in a firefight. Many other military and government leaders were killed or captured at this time. On December 13, 2003, the biggest prize of all came when Saddam himself was found alive at the bottom of a hole near Tikrit, in the Sunni Triangle.

However, the violent backlash against the coalition forces was increasing. Many **Shi'ite** Iraqis had welcomed the Americans as liberators at first, but now they saw them as an army of **occupation**. In the spring of 2004, there was a major Shi'ite uprising. At its head was a militia called the Mahdi Army, led by Moqtada al-Sadr.

The Mahdi Army launched a series of riots, bombings, and assaults in the southern and eastern parts of the country. Its targets were not just coalition troops, but also the newly recruited Iraqi soldiers and police who were being trained by the United States. At the same time, Sunni insurgents were fighting a major battle against U.S. forces in the town of Fallujah, north of Baghdad.

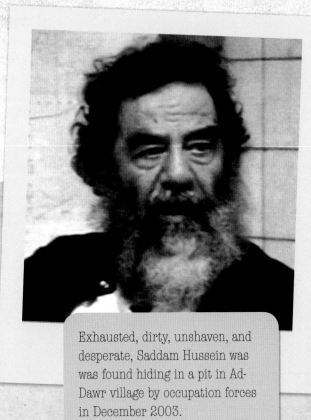

Death of a dictator

Saddam Hussein was handed over to the Iraqi authorities in June 2004. He went on trial in an Iraqi court in July 2004, and on October 19, 2005, he was found guilty of committing crimes against humanity during his time as president. On November 5, 2006, he was sentenced to death by hanging. The execution was carried out on December 30.

Exhausted, dirty, unshaven, and desperate, Saddam Hussein was was found hiding in a pit in Ad-Dawr village by occupation forces in December 2003.

Another WMD hunt

Meanwhile, inspectors from the United States, United Kingdom, and Australia had been searching the country for evidence to prove that Saddam had WMDs. They were part of the Iraq Survey Group (ISG), which replaced the UN inspection teams. The ISG's first report in October 2003 stated that no weapons had been found. Many people in the United States and United Kingdom were shocked. Their governments had given the threat of Iraq's WMDs as a major reason for going to war.

The ISG's final report appeared on October 6, 2004, and it provided more uncomfortable reading for Bush and Blair. It concluded that Saddam's WMDs were "essentially destroyed in 1991" (after the Gulf War), and that by the time of the invasion Saddam had no plans to develop more.[3]

Bush was defiant, telling reporters the next day, "Based on all the information we have today, I believe we were right to take action."[4] But bad news was piling up. Only days earlier, it was publicly announced that the total number of Americans killed during and after the invasion had passed 1,000.[5] But despite growing criticism, Bush was re-elected as US president on November 2.

Abu Ghraib

After the invasion, U.S. forces held suspected terrorists in Abu Ghraib prison, in Baghdad. During 2004, newspapers reported evidence of horrific abuse suffered by prisoners at the hands of U.S. soldiers. This included torture, beatings, rape, and even murder. The stories, accompanied by graphic photos, shocked the world and shamed the United States, and it caused much violence and anger among Iraqis. Many came to believe that the U.S. occupation was as bad as Saddam's regime. The culprits were tried and were themselves imprisoned, though some thought their sentences were too lenient.

A violent new year

The beginning of 2005 brought even more bloodshed. By now, Shi'ite and Sunni factions (small, organized groups) were fighting each other as well as the occupying troops and the new Iraqi security forces. The country's insurgents were also joined by a growing number of Islamist terrorists from abroad, including members of al-Qaeda and others backed by neighbouring Iran. They had come to take part in the fight against the Americans.

Car bombs, suicide bombs, IEDs, and rocket and gun attacks killed dozens of people and wounded hundreds more every month. Rebels assassinated the governor of Baghdad on January 4. Thirty-seven US personnel were killed in an explosion and a helicopter crash on January 26.[6] But most of the dead were Iraqi civilians.

However, January 30 saw a sign of a possibly brighter future. Over eight million Iraqi adults (more than half of the total eligible) went to the polling booths to vote in the first post-Saddam election of a parliament. The result was a victory for the two Shi'ite parties and the Kurdish independence party. Sunni candidates gained very few votes, mainly because Sunnis boycotted (refused to participate in) the vote.

President Bush, as he had promised, had turned Iraq into a state with a democratically elected government. But how democratic and successful was it?

- Many believed that US officials had too much control over the election process and influenced the result.

- Most Iraqi Sunnis refused to vote, partly because they resented measures taken against the Ba'ath Party.

- Many people did not vote because of the threat of violence from insurgents. In total, there were 300 attacks on polling stations, causing over 40 deaths.[7]

Suicide bombings by insurgents killed and wounded thousands of people—the vast majority of them innocent Iraqi civilians. This photo shows the aftermath of a suicide truck bombing which killed 22 people and wounded many more.

After the end of combat operations, a new Iraqi army was recruited. Its troops were trained by U.S. and British soldiers.

Losing control

Despite the elections, violence continued to rise throughout 2005. By the fall, the US death toll reached 2,000. A CIA report concluded that the war had not only failed to stop the spread of terrorism, but it had also actually turned Iraq into a new haven for terrorists, especially al-Qaeda.[8]

The Green Zone

International officials and military chiefs lived in a private compound in central Baghdad. This was known as the Green Zone, or "the Bubble," because it kept them isolated from ordinary Iraqis. The zone was surrounded by "T-Walls" (reinforced and blast-proof concrete slabs), chain fences, and razor wire, and it had entries through armed checkpoints.[10] It was attacked by insurgents several times with shells, mortars, and suicide bombs.

The US-led forces seemed to be losing the war, and opinion in the United States was turning against the president. A poll found that 58 per cent of Americans doubted his honesty. Yet Bush was still defiant. On November 30, he told an audience: "We will never back down, never give in, and never accept anything less than complete victory."[9]

Civil war

On February 22, 2006, two huge bombs destroyed the Golden Mosque in Samarra, one of the holiest sites for Shi'ite Muslims. The bombers were Sunni extremists, linked to al-Qaeda. This act enraged Iraq's Shi'ite majority. One Shi'ite leader told Bush, "This is the equivalent of your 9/11."[11]

The bombing sparked an even more savage civil war in Iraq, centered mainly on the area around Baghdad. This was not just between two sides of Islam, which included Sunni supporters of the old Saddam regime and Shi'ite militias such as the Mahdi Army. Smaller sects and organizations were also involved, some of which attacked others at random, in addition to the U.S.-led occupiers. These included Iraqi nationalists who wanted Iraq to decide its own future, foreign jihadists such as al-Qaeda, and forces backed by Iran.

Nouri al-Maliki

The chaos of the civil war was made worse by the fact that Iraq's rival political parties had failed to form a government or choose a prime minister. In May 2006, President Bush decided to take action. He believed Iraq needed strong leadership and ordered his staff in Baghdad to put pressure on Iraqi politicians to select a leader. They quickly chose a man named Nouri al-Maliki.

Bush's change of plan

By late 2006, it was clear the coalition armies and the newly trained Iraqi security forces were unable to cope with the scale of the violence. Several regions and towns were under the control of insurgent militias. According to UN figures, 6,599 Iraqi civilians were killed in July and August alone.[12] Then, on one day—November 23—at least 161 people died in a single Sunni bombing attack in Baghdad.[13]

Three years after the invasion, President Bush realized a simple truth: the U.S. army of occupation in Iraq was not big enough. At this time, there were about 127,000 U.S. troops in the country and 7,000 UK troops.[14] On January 10, 2007, Bush announced a "surge" in numbers. More than 20,000 extra soldiers and Marines would be sent to Iraq.

Getting out

The U.S. surge gradually reduced the amount of sectarian violence (violence related to a single sect) in southern and eastern Iraq. But it was too late. Many people were pushing for a complete withdrawal of coalition forces. In February, Blair announced that nearly half the UK force would be going home. In May, the Iraqi parliament demanded that the United States draw up a timetable for leaving. Most people believed the presence of the United States and United Kingdom was now provoking violence, not preventing it.

The process took a long time. The UK units finished combat operations in Iraq on April 30, 2009. But it was not until December 2011 that the U.S. government declared that the war was officially over. The last U.S. troops left Iraq on December 18 and crossed the border into Kuwait. One soldier said: "The Iraqis are going to wake up in the morning and no one will be there."[15]

In 2009, six years after the fall of Baghdad, thousands of Shi'ite supporters of the radical cleric Moqtada al-Sadr protested against the continued U.S. presence in Iraq.

Blair and Bush leave office

Long before the coalition forces had left Iraq, the two main leaders of the invasion had left office. Tony Blair resigned as UK prime minister on June 27, 2007, and was replaced by Gordon Brown (the former chancellor of the exchequer, responsible for the United Kingdom's finances). George W. Bush's presidency ended on January 20, 2009. The new president was Barack Obama.

The Legacy of the War

The U.S.-led invasion of Iraq took just six weeks. But the war and unrest that followed lasted for more than eight years, and the violence continues to this day. The main decision to begin the conflict was made by one man, George W. Bush. He might not have made that decision without Tony Blair, who decided to pledge his support. This meant that the United States was not internationally isolated. What is the legacy of these decisions made about Iraq and the rest of the world? And what effect did they have on the reputations of Bush and Blair?

There are a number of different ways to assess the legacy of Iraq.

Deaths and injuries

Nobody kept an official count of the number of civilian Iraqis who were killed or injured during the war. One reliable source has calculated the total of dead at over 115,000. There must also be a huge (but unknown) tally of people wounded or maimed (wounded with permanent damage). It is estimated that at least 60 percent of Iraqi children suffered psychological problems due to their experience of the violence.[1]

Casualty figures

The following chart shows the number of casualties resulting from the invasion, through December 2011:

Group	Total number of casualties
Iraqi civilians (deaths from violence)	106,905–116,785 deaths[6] (wounded figure unknown)
Iraqi military	46,000 deaths[7] (wounded figure unknown)
U.S. military	4,409 deaths; 31,927 wounded[8]
UK military	179 deaths; 5,970 wounded[9]

Refugees

By 2007, over 2 million Iraqis had fled to other countries to escape the horrors of the invasion and insurgency. Another 1.9 million had left their homes but stayed in Iraq.[2] Many have since gone back. But even in 2012, the UN Refugee Agency said there were still over 1 million displaced people in Iraq who could not return to their home regions due to fear of violence.[3]

More than 2 million Iraqi refugees left their homes and sought shelter abroad from the violence and destruction.

Wrecked infrastructure

The invasion of 2003 caused massive damage to Baghdad's water and electricity supplies, its sewage systems, and its roads and other transportation systems. US and UK bombs and missiles destroyed vast numbers of buildings, including houses, mosques, and schools. Bombing and shelling during the insurgency caused further damage.

Wrecked economy

In 2003, Iraq's economy was already weak due to years of US **sanctions** and Saddam's wars. But the long period of violence and unrest following the invasion made it much worse. Manufacturing, agriculture, and other industries were unable to function. The biggest blow was to the vital oil industry. Before 2003, Iraq was producing about 3.5 million barrels a day, but by 2007 this had fallen to 2 million.[4]

Cluster bombs

U.S. and UK forces hit Iraq with more than 29,000 bombs and missiles between March and May 2003.[10] Over 10,000 of these were cluster bombs, each of which spread as many as 200 "bomblets" over a wide area.[11] Many failed to explode right away and ended up killing or maiming people for months after the attacks. Young children were especially vulnerable, as the bomblets looked like shiny toys. At least 363 people were killed by cluster bombs in this three-month period.[12]

State failure

Between 2005 and 2008, Iraq was rated as one of the top five "failed states" in the world. A failed state is one with a weak government that has no firm control over its territories, widespread corruption, massive movement of refugees, ongoing economic decline, lack of public services, and frequent violations of human rights.[5]

The legacy in the United States

The legacy of the invasion of Iraq can also be examined in terms of the legacy it has left in the United States.

Deaths and injuries

More than 4,400 US soldiers died in the conflict (see page 44). Huge numbers of personnel have also been disabled or traumatized by the war and then discharged from the forces. Many have major psychiatric (related to the mind), social, and financial problems. Figures from 2012 also show that suicide rates among US soldiers have leaped by 80 per cent since the invasion began.[13]

Though the U.S. military withdrew from Iraq in 2011, its forces were not due to leave Afghanistan until 2014.

Loss of respect

The eagerness of the United States to go to war, and the crushing force of the invasion, made it very unpopular in many parts of the world. As the war dragged on, the US government lost more respect because it failed to control or reconstruct Iraq, and because it had no effective plans for withdrawal and handing over the country to an effective Iraqi government. In 2007, a BBC poll throughout the world showed that 73 per cent of people disapproved of the US government's handling of Iraq.[14] On top of this, the uncovering of widespread torture and other abuses of prisoners, and of unprovoked attacks on civilians by the US military, led to calls for many people to be tried for war crimes.

The legacy in the United Kingdom

The invasion of Iraq has also left a legacy in the United Kingdom.

Deaths and injuries

The United Kingdom suffered over 6,000 casualties during the war. Many people who fought in Iraq also suffered physical and

The cost of war

What was the financial cost of the Iraq War?

- United States: The war has cost the United States over $800 billion.[18] Some believe the eventual total (including replacing equipment, costs in maintaining order in Iraq, and the care of ex-soldiers) will be at least $4 trillion.[19]

- United Kingdom: The war has cost the United Kingdom over $14 billion.[20]

mental stress caused by their experiences. About 20 per cent of veterans experience depression, and 13 per cent have alcohol and drug problems.[15]

Mistrust of politicians
Investigations since the war have shown how much the UK government used misleading or wrong information in its campaign to "sell" the invasion to the public. This, together with the horrors and mistakes of the occupation itself, made many people angry with politicians (from both major parties, Labour and Conservative) who voted for the war in March 2003. In 2006, a survey found that three-quarters of the UK population did not trust cabinet ministers to tell the truth.[16]

The global legacy

The invasion of Iraq has also left a legacy worldwide.

Growth of terrorism
George W. Bush launched a war on terror, yet the invasion on Iraq actually increased the spread of terrorism. Al-Qaeda and other organizations used the chaos of the insurgency to establish themselves in Iraq. Resentment of US actions in Iraq has increased the number of radical Muslims throughout the world.

Political instability in the Middle East
The US invasion caused some Middle Eastern countries to become more aggressive against Israel, which is a strong ally of the United States. Among the hostile countries was Iran. Iran has backed fundamentalist Shi'ite groups in Lebanon and Syria.[17]

Failure in Afghanistan
The Iraq War diverted attention (and troops) away from the ongoing conflict in Afghanistan. This gave the Taliban a chance to rebuild its campaign against the coalition forces and the new Afghan government.

The Iraq effect: George W. Bush

At the start of his first term in office, George W. Bush outlined his ambitious plans. These included new measures related to health care, social security, and immigration. But the tragedy of 9/11 changed his course completely. 9/11 was a catastrophe in U.S. history, and the president felt he had to concentrate on the defense and security of his homeland and the prevention of further terrorist attacks. Did he make the right decision about Iraq?

In September 2001, just after the 9/11 attacks, President Bush set a record. An opinion poll showed he was the most popular president since polls began. Of those questioned, 90 percent approved of what he was doing. In April 2008, Bush set another record. He became the most unpopular president since polls began. His approval rating had fallen to 28 percent, while 69 percent of Americans disapproved of his performance.[21]

There were several reasons for this slump, including Bush's handling of the U.S. economy. But by far the biggest reason was the Iraq War. Several journalists called him "the worst U.S. president in history." International groups, including Amnesty International, suggested that another country could legally arrest Bush for war crimes (notably for allowing torture). This may have caused Bush to cancel a European trip in February 2011.[22] He now rarely travels outside the United States.

The Iraq effect: Tony Blair

In many ways, Tony Blair was a very successful leader. He took the Labour Party to three election victories in a row, and he was UK prime minister for 10 years. His governments passed laws ensuring a minimum wage and greater freedom of information, in addition to giving independent parliaments to Scotland and Wales. Blair was closely involved in the 1998 Good Friday Agreement, a milestone in the peace process in Northern Ireland.

However, he will be mainly remembered for his decision to join Bush's invasion of Iraq. Public opposition to the war was much stronger in the United Kingdom than in the United States, and Blair quickly lost popularity. As early as August 26, 2004, notable people, including 11 members of Parliament, tried to have him "impeached" (tried in court) for misleading the public over Iraq. The move failed.[23] By March 2006, a poll showed his approval rating had fallen to only 28 percent.[24]

Since Blair left Parliament, there have been several attempts to have him charged with war crimes, and he has faced repeated protests and demonstrations. In January 2011, he provided evidence at a major UK inquiry into the Iraq War, chaired by John Chilcot. (Blair had previously appeared there a year earlier.) There were loud protests against him both inside and outside the building. The mother of a dead soldier told him: "Your lies killed our son. I hope you can live with it."[25]

Decisive words: Suffering doubt

"Don't believe anyone who tells you when they receive letters like that they don't suffer any doubt."

> Tony Blair, after receiving hate mail from families of soldiers killed in Iraq, September 2003[27]

In 2011, Tony Blair was called to give evidence to the Chilcot Inquiry into the conduct of the Iraq invasion. Many people wanted to charge him with war crimes.

What Might Have Been Different?

The Iraq War has changed our world in many ways. But what would have happened if George W. Bush and Tony Blair had decided not to invade Iraq—or to make different decisions after they had invaded? How different might the course of history have been? And would many thousands of lives have been saved?

What if Bush and his advisers had not been so determined to topple Saddam?

If Bush and his advisers had not been so determined to topple Saddam, they might have waited longer before deciding on an all-out military attack. They might also have believed the findings of the weapons inspectors, which showed that there was no evidence of WMDs. The UN was actively trying to solve the Saddam problem by peaceful means. Sanctions were having a big effect on Iraq and causing widespread hardship. But could this approach have forced Saddam to quit or led to a popular uprising against him?

What if Iraq had not been such a weak enemy?

If Iraq had not been such a weak enemy, the U.S.-led coalition might not have been in such a rush to invade in the first place. The respected British journalist Patrick Cockburn wrote: "The main motive for going to war was that the White House thought it could win such a conflict very easily."[1] As it turned out, the invasion was the only easy part.

The very last U.S. military base on Iraqi soil, Camp Adder, closed on November 17, 2011. The troops crossed the border into Kuwait early the next morning.

What if Blair had not supported the U.S. plans?

If Blair had not supported the U.S. plans, the war might never have taken place. President Bush was reluctant to have the United States go it alone in Iraq. He needed strong support from another Western nation. Without Blair's help, would he have been forced to delay his decision?

What if the UK House of Commons had voted against the invasion?

If the House of Commons had voted against the invasion, Blair would not have had the power to send UK troops to Iraq. So, possibly, U.S. forces would not have gone without this additional support. Why didn't more members of Parliament vote against war, given the strength of feeling in the United Kingdom? Many were clearly convinced by the unreliable information presented to the government and felt it would be "unpatriotic" to vote against the invasion.

What do you think?:

Could history have been changed?

Do you agree with the suggested answers to the "What if?" questions? Or do you have a better response? Select one of the topics on these pages to study further. You may need to do more research first.

What if the United States had stationed a much stronger armed force in occupied Iraq and had clearer plans for rebuilding the country?

If the United States had used stronger forces and had clearer plans for rebuilding Iraq, it would have been able to prevent the breakdown into insurgency and civil war. It would also have been able to rebuild Iraq more quickly. What were the reasons for sending a relatively small number of soldiers? Coalition leaders had believed, mistakenly, that Iraqis would be more united once Saddam was removed.

What if the war had never taken place?

If the war had never taken place, Iraqis might have overthrown Saddam without outside help. Then, Iraq might have made a more peaceful transition from dictatorship to democracy. It would have taken longer and would still have caused much suffering, but there would have been much less international anger against the United States.

Conclusion

The decisions made by George W. Bush and Tony Blair are part of history. So, was the invasion of Iraq a success or a failure? Or is it still too early to judge? In 2003, Bush said it would take about 10 years to understand the impact and significance of the war.[1]

Beliefs and decisions

But what causes people to make one decision rather than another? Bush and Blair, like most world leaders, had strong political and spiritual beliefs, and they followed them—in spite of conflicting evidence. With hindsight, it is easy to see what went wrong. But could the resulting disaster have been predicted?

On the next page is a brief summary of the main events and the decisions that triggered them.

What do you think?:

Were there any positive results of the Iraq War?

Supporters of U.S. and UK actions in Iraq point to at least three good effects:

- The end of Saddam Hussein: The invasion destroyed Saddam's long and brutal regime and gave the Iraqi people a chance to elect their own government.

- The "Arab Spring": The fall of one Middle Eastern dictator encouraged people in the region to rise up against their leaders (in Tunisia, Libya, Egypt, and Syria). At the same time, Western nations had learned lessons from the disastrous invasion of Iraq and so behaved very differently. They supported opposition parties but did not send troops (which would have made them seem like invaders). And they acted with UN support.

- No repeat of 9/11: The "war on terror" has worked—at least in the United States, where there have been no more major terrorist acts since 9/11.

What do you think? Are these positive points for Bush and Blair? Find out more about the topics mentioned, such as the Arab Spring, and decide if you agree or disagree. Can you discover or think of any other positive results of the war?

Try this site and others like it:

www.usatoday.com/news/world/iraq/2006-03-16-iraq-war-anniversary-effects_x.htm.

The Bushes: Father and son

George H. W. Bush—George W. Bush's father—was president during the Gulf War of 1991. After defeating the Iraqi forces, he decided not to pursue Saddam Hussein and overthrow him. Throughout the rest of the 1990s, the U.S. government saw Saddam as a continued threat to world peace. He was accused of possessing or developing weapons of mass destruction.

George W. Bush became president in 2001. The horrific attacks of 9/11 showed him the dangers posed by world terrorism. Bush announced the start of a "war on terror," led by the United States, and sent troops into Afghanistan, which was seen as a haven for Islamist groups such as al-Qaeda.

Bush also regarded Iraq as a terrorist base, despite a lack of evidence. He was determined not to make the same mistake as his father. He ordered plans to be prepared for an invasion and found strong support from the UK prime minister, Tony Blair. Inspectors were unable to find any WMDs in Iraq, and the UN would not approve direct military action.

The United States and United Kingdom decided to invade anyway. On March 19, 2003, coalition forces attacked Iraq, and within a few weeks they had captured Baghdad. U.S. forces set up a temporary governing body, which disbanded the Iraqi armed forces and police. This led to an explosion of looting, destruction, and unrest. Saddam was captured in December.

During 2004, tensions between ethnic groups led to a spiral of bloodshed. Thousands died in bombings, riots, and other violence. The U.S. and UK occupying force was too small to keep control. Islamist hatred of the United States increased quickly, and terrorist fighters from other countries arrived to increase the chaos. By 2006, a confused civil war was raging.

That winter, Bush decided to send more U.S. forces in a "troop surge" to impose order. But by now, the new Iraqi government wanted the occupiers to leave, and the conflict had made Bush and Blair highly unpopular at home. Both left office by 2009. UK forces ceased combat operations in the same year, and the last U.S. troops withdrew in December 2011.

Timeline

1990
August 2
Iraqi forces invade Kuwait

1991
January 17
Operation Desert Storm begins, as U.S. and other coalition forces drive Saddam out of Kuwait

1991
March 10
A cease-fire is agreed upon; coalition forces do not invade Iraq

1991
April
UN weapons inspectors find evidence of WMDs

2002
October 11
The U.S. Congress votes to authorize the use of military force against Iraq

2002
July 23
Blair meets with secret service and intelligence chiefs in Downing Street

2002
April 6
Blair visits Bush and pledges support for a war against Saddam

2002
January 29
President Bush refers to an "axis of evil" in his State of the Union address

2001
October 7
The U.S. coalition invasion of Afghanistan begins

2003
February 3
The Blair government publishes the Iraq dossier (or "dodgy dossier")

2003
February 23
The UN Security Council rejects a new resolution on Iraq

2003
March 17
President Bush gives Saddam 48 hours to leave Iraq

2003
March 18
The UK House of Commons votes for war

2005
January 30
Iraqis vote in an election to form a new government; violence between ethnic groups increases

2004
November 7
The Battle of Fallujah is fought

2004
November 2
George W. Bush is elected for a second term

2004
October 6
The Iraq Survey Group reports that no WMDs were discovered

2006
February 22
Bombs destroy the Golden Mosque in Samarra

2006
April onward
Violence increases further, as civil war spreads across much of Iraq

2006
December 30
Saddam Hussein is executed

2007
January 23
President Bush announces a military "surge," with 20,000 extra troops

2007
June 27
Blair resigns as UK prime minister after 10 years in power

1993

January 20
Bill Clinton
succeeds George
H. W. Bush as
U.S. president

1993

February 26
The first terrorist
attacks take place
on the World
Trade Center, in
New York

1997

May 2
The Labour Party wins
the general election in
the United Kingdom;
Tony Blair becomes
prime minister

1998

August 7
Al-Qaeda bombs
U.S. embassies
in East Africa

2001

September 11
Terrorist attacks by al-
Qaeda destroy the World
Trade Center and damage
the Pentagon; nearly
3,000 people are killed

2001

January 20
George W.
Bush succeeds
Clinton as U.S.
president

1998

**December
16–19**
The Operation
Desert Fox air
strikes occur on
Iraq

1998

December 15
UN arms
inspections are
stopped after
obstruction from
Saddam

2003

March 19
Renewed air
strikes begin
against Baghdad

2003

March 20
U.S. and UK
coalition forces
invade Iraq

2003

April 6
UK forces enter
Basra

2003

April 9
U.S. forces
take control of
Baghdad

2003

May 1
Bush announces
that major
fighting is over

2004

April 28
Revelations of
abuse at Abu
Ghraib prison
are revealed

2004

Spring
The Shi'ite
insurgency
begins

2003

December 13
Saddam Hussein
is captured near
Tikrit

2003

July
The Sunni
insurgency
begins

2003

May 23
Paul Bremer
disbands the
Iraqi military

2008

November 4
Barack Obama is elected
U.S. president; Bush
continues to stay in
office and run the Iraq
War until Obama's
inauguration

2009

January 20
Barack Obama is
inaugurated U.S.
president

2009

April 30
UK forces
end combat
operations in
Iraq

2011

December 18
The last U.S.
forces withdraw
from Iraq

Notes on Sources

Fighting Saddam (pages 4–5)

1. The White House, "Operation Iraqi Freedom: President Bush Addresses the Nation," March 19, 2003, http://georgewbush-whitehouse.archives.gov/news/releases/2003/03/20030319-17.html.

2. Bob Woodward, *Plan of Attack* (London: Pocket Books, 2004), 401.

3. Spartacus Educational, "Saddam Hussein," http://www.spartacus.schoolnet.co.uk/IRQsaddam.htm.

4. Christopher Dickey and Evan Thomas, "How Saddam Happened," The Daily Beast, September 22, 2002, http://www.thedailybeast.com/newsweek/2002/09/22/how-saddam-happened.html.

Prior History (pages 6–9)

1. Council on Foreign Relations, "UN Security Council Resolution 678, Iraq/Kuwait," http://www.cfr.org/un/un-security-council-resolution-678-iraq-kuwait/p11205?breadcrumb=%2Fregion%2F408%2Fkuwait.

2. Central Intelligence Agency, "The World Fact Book," https://www.cia.gov/library/publications/the-world-factbook/geos/xx.html.

3. Central Intelligence Agency, "The World Fact Book: Oil Production," https://www.cia.gov/library/publications/the-world-factbook/fields/2173.html#xx.

4. Joel Connelly, "In the Northwest: Bush-Cheney Flip-Flops Costs American Blood," *Seattle Post-Intelligencer*, September 28, 2004, http://www.seattlepi.com/news/article/In-the-Northwest-Bush-Cheney-flip-flops-cost-1155271.php.

Saddam, Terrorism, and 9/11 (pages 10–17)

1. John Keegan, *The Iraq War* (London: Hutchinson, 2004), 84.

2. Brian Jones, *Failing Intelligence: The True Story of How We Were Fooled into Going to War in Iraq* (London: Biteback Publishing, 2010), 27.

3. U.S. Department of State, "U.S. Relations with Iraq," September 7, 2012, http://www.state.gov/r/pa/ei/bgn/6804.htm.

4. BBC News, "Iraqi Leader's Koran 'Written in Blood,'" September 25, 2000, http://news.bbc.co.uk/1/hi/world/monitoring/media_reports/941490.stm.

5. James Bamford, *A Pretext for War: 9/11, Iraq and the Abuse of America's Intelligence Agencies* (New York: Anchor Books, 2005), 264.

6. PBS Online News Hour, "African Embassy Bombings," http://www.pbs.org/newshour/bb/africa/embassy_bombing/map.html.

7. Twentieth Century Atlas, "Minor Atrocities of the Twentieth Century," http://users.erols.com/mwhite28/warstat7.htm#Iraq98.

8. Bartleby, "George W. Bush: First Inaugural Address," http://www.bartleby.com/124/pres66.html.

9. Jason Burke, *Al-Qaeda: The True Story of Radical Islam* (London: Penguin, 2004), 3.

The Road to War (pages 18–23)

1. George W. Bush, *Decision Points* (London: Virgin Books, 2011), 140.

2. Joel Roberts, "Plans for Iraq Attack Began on 9/11," CBS News, September 10, 2009, http://www.cbsnews.com/stories/2002/09/04/september11/main520830.shtml.

3. Richard Clarke, *Against All Enemies: Inside America's War on Terror* (New York: Free Press, 2004), quoted in OntheIssues.org, http://www.issues2000.org/Archive/Against_All_Enemies_War_+_Peace.htm.

4. *Washington Post*, "Text: President Bush Addresses the Nation," September 20, 2001, http://www.washingtonpost.com/wp-srv/nation/specials/attacked/transcripts/bushaddress_092001.html.

5. *New York Times*, "The Guantánamo Project," http://projects.nytimes.com/guantanamo/about.

6. Keegan, *The Iraq War*, 99.

7. CNN, "Bush State of the Union Address," January 29, 2002, http://articles.cnn.com/2002-01-29/politics/bush.speech.txt_1_firefighter-returns-terrorist-training-camps-interim-leader/4?_s=PM:ALLPOLITICS.

8. FBI, "Most Wanted Terrorists: Usama Bin Laden," http://www.fbi.gov/wanted/wanted_terrorists/usama-bin-laden.

9. Bush, *Decision Points*, 232.

10. Tony Blair, *A Journey* (London: Hutchinson, 2010), 380.

11. James Risen, *State of War: The Secret History of the CIA and the Bush Administration* (London: Pocket Books, 2007), 86.

12. Woodward, *Plan of Attack*, 294.

13. The White House, "George W. Bush Delivers Graduation Speech at West Point," June 1, 2002, http://georgewbush-whitehouse.archives.gov/news/releases/2002/06/print/20020601-3.html.

14. Woodward, *Plan of Attack*, 119.

Decision Time (pages 24–29)

1. Blair, *A Journey*, 400.

2. Jones, *Failing Intelligence*, 69.

3. The Downing Street Memos, "Text of the Original 'Downing Street Memo,'" http://downingstreetmemo.com/memos.html.

4. Woodward, *Plan of Attack*, 148.

5. *Ibid.*, 150.

6. Bush, *Decision Points*, 239.

7. Woodward, *Plan of Attack*, 178.

8. Bamford, *A Pretext for War*, 319.

9. *Ibid.*, 326.

10. Risen, *State of War*, 116.

11. Woodward, *Plan of Attack*, 240.

12. Bamford, A *Pretext for War*, 360.

13. Woodward, *Plan of Attack*, 338.

14. *The Guardian*, "Full text: Tony Blair's speech," March 17, 2003, http://www.guardian.co.uk/politics/2003/mar/18/foreignpolicy.iraq1.

15. Blair, *A Journey*, 439.

Shock and Awe (pages 30–35)

1. CNN, "War in Iraq: Forces, U.S. Coalition and Coalition/U.S. Army," http://edition.cnn.com/SPECIALS/2003/iraq/forces/coalition/army/index.html.

2. Bush, *Decision Points*, 254.

3. Woodward, *Plan of Attack*, 399

4. Woodward, *Plan of Attack*, 403.

5. BBC News, "Massive Air Raids Rock Iraq," March 21, 2003, http://news.bbc.co.uk/1/hi/world/middle_east/2873811.stm#map.

6. Woodward, *Plan of Attack*, 407.

7. Blair, *A Journey*, 445.

8. Bush, *Decision Points*, 256.

9. The White House, "Operation Iraqi Freedom: President Bush Announces Major Combat Operations in Iraq Have Ended," May 1, 2003, http://georgewbush-whitehouse.archives.gov/news/releases/2003/05/20030501-15.html.

10. Judy Keen, "Bush to Troops: Mission Accomplished," USA Today, June 5, 2003, http://www.usatoday.com/news/world/iraq/2003-06-05-bush-qatar_x.htm.

11. icasualties, "Iraq Coalition Casualties: Fatalities By Year and Month," http://www.icasualties.org/Iraq/ByMonth.aspx.

12. Carl Conetta, "The Wages of War: Iraqi Combatant and Noncombatant Fatalities in the 2003 Conflict," Project on Defense Alternatives, http://www.comw.org/pda/0310rm8.html.

13. Iraq Body Count, "Documented Civilian Deaths from Violence," http://www.iraqbodycount.org/.

The Bloody Years (pages 36–43)

1. Risen, *State of War*, 133.

2. Jane Arraf, "U.S. Dissolves Iraq Army, Defense and Information Ministries," CNN, May 23, 2003, http://articles.cnn.com/2003-05-23/world/sprj.nitop.army.dissolve_1_new-iraqi-corps-iraqi-army-saddam-regime?_s=PM:WORLD.

3. Michael Isikoff and David Corn, *Hubris* (New York: Three Rivers Press, 2006), 374.

4. *Ibid.*, 375.

5. Bamford, *A Pretext for War*, 397.

6. Isikoff and Corn, *Hubris*, 380.

7. Kenneth Katzman, "Iraq: Elections, Government, and Constitution," U.S. Department of State, November 20, 2006, http://fpc.state.gov/documents/organization/76838.pdf.

8. Risen, *State of War*, 219–20.

9. Isikoff and Corn, *Hubris*, 395.

10. GlobalSecurity, "Green Zone," http://www.globalsecurity.org/military/world/iraq/baghdad-green-zone.htm.

11. Bush, *Decision Points*, 361.

12. Anthony H. Cordesman, "Is There a 'Civil War' in Iraq?" Center for Strategic and International Studies, http://csis.org/files/media/csis/pubs/061016_iraq_civil.pdf.

13. Associated Press, "Bombs, Mortars in Shiite Slum Kill at Least 161," MSNBC, November 23, 2006, http://www.msnbc.msn.com/id/15866123/.

14. Michael R. Gordon, "U.S. General in Iraq Outlines Troop Cuts," *New York Times*, June 25, 2006, http://www.nytimes.com/2006/06/25/world/middleeast/25military.html?_r=1&pagewanted=all.

15. Greg Jaffe, "Last U.S. Troops Cross Iraqi Border into Kuwait," *Washington Post*, December 17, 2011, http://www.washingtonpost.com/world/national-security/last-us-troops-cross-iraqi-border-into-kuwait/2011/12/17/gIQArEyX1O_story.html.

The Legacy of the War (pages 44–49)

1. IRIN, "IRAQ: Traumatised Iraqi children suffer psychological damage," http://www.irinnews.org/Report/73258/IRAQ-Traumatised-Iraqi-children-suffer-psychological-damage.

2. Nir Rosen, "The Flight from Iraq," May 13, 2007, *New York Times*, http://www.nytimes.com/2007/05/13/magazine/13refugees-t.html?pagewanted=all.

3. The UN Refugee Agency, "2012 UNHCR Country Operations Profile: Iraq," http://www.unhcr.org/cgi-bin/texis/vtx/page?page=49e486426&submit=GO.

4. *The Independent*, "Blood and Oil: How the West Will Profit from Iraq's Most Precious Commodity," January 7, 2007, http://www.independent.co.uk/news/world/middle-east/blood-and-oil-how-the-west-will-profit-from-iraqs-most-precious-commodity-431119.html.

5. The Fund for Peace, "The Failed States Index 2007," http://www.fundforpeace.org/global/?q=fsi-grid2007.

6. Iraq Body Count, "Documented Civilian Deaths from Violence."

7. Iraq Body Count, "Iraq Deaths from Violence, 2003–2011," http://www.iraqbodycount.org/analysis/numbers/2011/.

8. U.S. Department of Defense, "Casualty Status Fatalities," http://www.defense.gov/news/casualty.pdf.

9. Casualty Monitor, "British Casualties: Iraq," http://www.casualty-monitor.org/p/iraq.html.

10. Bamford, *A Pretext for War*, 379.

11. *Ibid.*, 392.

12. John Sloboda and Hamit Dardagan, "How Many Civilians Were Killed by Cluster Bombs?" Iraq Body Count, May 6, 2003, http://www.iraqbodycount.org/analysis/numbers/killed-by-cluster-bombs/.

13. Carrie Gann, "Suicides, Mental Health Woes Soar Since Start of Iraq War, Study Finds," ABC News, March 8, 2012, http://abcnews.go.com/Health/study-80-percent-army-suicides-start-iraq-war/story?id=15872301.

14. BBC News, "World View of U.S. Role Goes from Bad to Worse," January 3, 2007, http://news.bbc.co.uk/1/shared/bsp/hi/pdfs/23_01_07_us_poll.pdf.

15. Michael Scott Moore, "PTSD Affecting More U.S. Soldiers Than British," *Pacific Standard*, June 22, 2011, http://www.psmag.com/health/ptsd-affecting-more-american-soldiers-than-british-32096/.

16. Kirsty Walker, "Iraq War to Blame for Mistrust in Politicians," *Daily Mail*, September 15, 2006, http://www.dailymail.co.uk/news/article-405356/Iraq-war-blame-mistrust-politicians.html.

17. The Guardian, "Former MI5 chief delivers damning verdict on Iraq invasion" http://www.guardian.co.uk/uk/2010/jul/20/chilcot-mi5-boss-iraq-war?intcmp=239.

18. Cost of War, "Cost of War to the United States," http://costofwar.com/en/.

19. David R. Francis, "Iraq War Will Cost More Than World War II," *Christian Science Monitor*, October 25, 2011, http://www.csmonitor.com/Business/new-economy/2011/1025/Iraq-war-will-cost-more-than-World-War-II.

20. BBC News, "Iraq War in Figures," December 14, 2011, http://www.bbc.co.uk/news/world-middle-east-11107739.

21. Susan Page, "Disapproval of Bush Breaks Record," *USA Today*, April 22, 2008, http://www.usatoday.com/news/washington/2008-04-21-bushrating_N.htm.

22. Ewan MacAskill and Afua Hirsch, "George Bush Calls off Trip to Switzerland," *Guardian*, February 6, 2011, http://www.guardian.co.uk/law/2011/feb/06/george-bush-trip-to-switzerland.

23. BBC News, "Blair Impeachment Campaign Starts," August 27, 2004, http://news.bbc.co.uk/1/hi/uk_politics/3600438.stm.

24. Infowars, "Blair Approval Rating Falls to 28% in Britain," http://www.infowars.com/articles/world/uk_blair_approval_rating_falls_28_percent.htm.

25. Rosa Prince, "Chilcot Inquiry: Tony Blair Heckled as He Expresses Regret for This Loss of Life in the Iraq War," *The Telegraph*, January 21, 2011, http://www.telegraph.co.uk/news/politics/tony-blair/8274202/Chilcot-Inquiry-Tony-Blair-heckled-as-he-expresses-regret-for-this-loss-of-life-in-the-Iraq-war.html.

26. Woodward, *Plan of Attack*, 420.

27. Ibid., 420.

What Might Have Been Different? (pages 50–51)

1. Patrick Cockburn, *The Occupation: War and Resistance in Iraq* (London: Verso, 2007), 2.

Conclusion (pages 52–53)

1. Woodward, *Plan of Attack*, 443.

Glossary

al-Qaeda global Islamist terrorist organization which uses extreme violence to pursue its goals of violent worlwide *jihad* and the imposition of *sharia* law

Arab member of the Arabic-speaking people, many of whom live in the Arabian countries of the Middle East

assassination murder (usually of a prominent person)

casualty person who is killed or wounded

Central Intelligence Agency (CIA) civilian body, run by the American government, which gathers information from other countries which concern the interests of the USA

civilian person who is not in the armed forces

civil war armed conflict between two factions or groups in a single country

coalition alliance between parties or nations

defector someone who leaves his or her country after giving up loyalty to it

democracy government by the people, through an elected body

dictator leader of a country who has absolute power over its people

doctrine set way of thinking; a principle put forward for others to believe in

embassy building where ambassadors (representatives of a country) live and work in another country

ethnic belonging to a social group within a country or other social system

exile ban a peson from their own country

extremist person who uses or campaigns for extreme measures to get what he or she wants (especially in politics or religion)

Federal Bureau of Investigation (FBI) U.S. government agency which investigates major criminal activities throughout the country and gathers national intelligence

fundamentalist member of a movement or belief system which stresses strict obedience to a set of principles (such as a religious creed)

improvised explosive device (IED) homemade bomb, usually planted by terrorists

inauguration formal introduction to an office or position of power

intelligence secret information, usually about an enemy

Islam world religion based on the teachings of the Prophet Muhammad and worshiping one God

Islamic to do with the religion of Islam

Islamist someone who works to promote the spread of Islam *jihad* Arabic word for "struggle"; though many Muslims use this word to describe forms of peaceful, spiritual struggle, some extremists have used it to describe a holy war against nonbelievers

Kurdish relating to an ethnic Muslim group living on the borders of Iraq and Turkey

legacy something which is left by somebody for future generations

liberate free or release from something

militia unofficial volunteer army or band of fighters

mosque Muslim house of worship

Muslim follower of the Islamic faith

neoconservative (neocon) describes beliefs belonging to a group of people (literally "new conservatives") who are in favor of very conservative views on economics, foreign policy, and other matters. The movement began in opposition to what was seen as the "soft" liberal attitudes of the 1960s.

occupation stationing of military forces in a foreign country in order to keep control

parliament assembly of the political representatives of a nation, who govern that nation

peshmerga Kurdish fighters campaigning for an independent Kurdish state

preemptive stopping someone from doing something by taking action in advance

prime minister leader of the ruling party in a parliament

regime system of government or rule

republic country that has an elected head of state, such as a president, who is not a hereditary monarch (king or queen)

resolution formal statement announcing a decision about a course of action

sanction penalty measure taken by a country or group of countries against another that has violated international laws

sect group of people who follow an extreme political or religious movement

sharia moral code and religious laws of Islam, based on the word of god and the teachings of the Prophet Muhammad

Shi'a second-largest sect of Muslims, who follow Ali (son-in-law of the Prophet Muhammad) and his heirs and reject many Sunni beliefs

Shi'ite member of the Shi'a sect of Muslims

Sunni largest sect of Muslims, they follow the traditions of the first four caliphs (Muslim rulers) as rightful successors to the Prophet Muhammad

Taliban militant Islamist political group that ruled Afghanistan from 1996 to 2001 and is still a major influence on developments in Afghanistan

Find Out More

The Iraq War is a very recent event in world history. Historians are still looking at the evidence and sources and figuring out how to analyze and draw lessons from this major event. You can find a lot of raw material for research in books, films, and online—but few final judgments. Why not try drawing your own conclusions?

Books

Adams, Simon. *The Iraq War* (Secret History). Mankato, Minn.: Arcturus, 2010.

Arnold, James R. *Saddam Hussein's Iraq* (Dictatorships). Minneapolis: 21st Century, 2009.

Bingham, Jane. *The Gulf Wars with Iraq* (Living Through). Chicago: Heinemann Library, 2012.

Bush, George W. *Decision Points*. New York: Crown, 2010.

Mason, Paul. *The Iraq War* (Timelines). Mankato, Minn.: Arcturus, 2010.

Miller, Mara. *The Iraq War: A Controversial War in Perspective* (Issues in Focus Today). Berkeley Heights, N.J.: Enslow, 2011.

Souter, Gerry, and Janet Souter. *War in Afghanistan and Iraq*. New York: Scholastic, 2011.

Winter, Jeanette. *The Librarian of Basra: A True Story from Iraq*. New York: Harcourt, 2005.

DVDs

Fahrenheit 9/11 (Columbia TriStar Home Entertainment, 2004) Michael Moore's satirical documentary about George W. Bush and the rush to invade Iraq is both funny and shocking.

Frontline: Bush's War (PBS Home Video, 2008) The road to war is revealed in interviews with Bush and his staff as well as filmed speeches and meetings.

The Iraq War (The History Channel, 2008) This six-hour documentary is about the war, seen through the eyes of reporters stationed with U.S. forces.

Uncovered: The War on Iraq (Carolina Productions, 2005) This film is a calm but gripping examination of the Bush administration and its claims about going to war.

Voices of Iraq (Magnolia Home Entertainment, 2006) Hear from Iraqis themselves—of all ages and faiths—about what they think of Saddam, the invasion, and other recent events.

Web sites

ethemes.missouri.edu/themes/646
This University of Missouri site gives recommended links for all sorts of Iraq-related information.

kids.britannica.com/comptons/article-9574392/Iraq-War
This site offers a simple chronological introduction to the conflict.

www.leadingtowar.com/?gclid=CMnF9qr_zbACFY5pfAodA0jTVg
This hard-hitting web site (and an accompanying film) chronicle the path to the invasion and insurgency.

mit.edu/humancostiraq
Find balanced facts and views on the human cost of the Iraq War at this site.

www.pbs.org/newshour/extra/features/iraq Read stories, experiences, and views from young people about the war here.

Other topics to research

- The history of Iraq in the past 100 years.
- The history and development of Islam.
- Other wars in which the USA and UK were major allies.
- The huge importance of oil in the modern world.
- Is it ever right to interfere with the government of a foreign country?

Index